SHADOWS

THE DEPICTION OF CAST SHADOWS
IN WESTERN ART

SHADOWS

THE DEPICTION OF CAST SHADOWS
IN WESTERN ART

E.H. GOMBRICH

A companion volume to an exhibition at
The National Gallery

National Gallery Publications, London
Distributed by Yale University Press

ACKNOWLEDGEMENTS

The author wishes to thank Erika Langmuir, Diana Davies, Elizabeth McGrath, James Cahill, Mariëtte Haveman, Professor J. Stumpel and Leonie Gombrich. To his regret the book by Michael Baxandall, *Shadows and Enlightenment* (Yale 1995), appeared too late for him to profit from its insights.

This book was published to accompany an exhibition in the Sunley Room at
The National Gallery, London
26 April–18 June 1995
Supported by the Bernard Sunley Charitable Organisation

First published in Great Britain in 1995 by
National Gallery Publications Limited
5/6 Pall Mall East, London SW1Y 5BA

NGPL ISBN 1 85709 091 8
525189

British Library Cataloguing-in-Publication Data.
A catalogue record is available from the British Library.

Library of Congress Catalog Card Number: 94–73937

Editor: Diana Davies
Designed by Steve Russell

Printed and bound in Great Britain by
Butler and Tanner, Frome and London

Front jacket: Follower of Rembrandt, *A Man seated reading at a Table in a Lofty Room*, detail (Plate 33).
Back jacket: *Self Portrait of the Author in the Setting Sun* (Plate 3).

CONTENTS

Clair obscur dans un seul objet

Fig. 2.

Detail of an engraving from Roger de Piles, *Elémens de la Peinture Pratique,* Paris 1684.

'**Shadow:** The darkness created by opaque bodies on the opposite side of the illuminated part.'

'**Shadow:** In the language of painters it is generally understood to refer to the more or less dark colour which serves in painting to give relief to the representation by gradually becoming lighter. It is divided in three degrees called shadow, half-shadow and cast shadow. By **shadow** (*ombra*) is meant that which a body creates on itself, as for instance a sphere that has light on one part and gradually becomes half light and half dark, and that dark part is described as shadow (penumbra). **Half-shadow** (*mezz' ombra*) is called that area that is between light and the shadow through which the one passes to the other, as we have said, gradually diminishing little by little according to the roundness of the object. **Cast shadow** (*sbattimento*) is the shadow that is caused on the ground or elsewhere by the depicted object...'

(After Filippo Baldinucci, *Vocabulario Toscano dell'Arte del Disegno,* Florence 1681.)

FOREWORD

Like every art historian of my generation, my way of thinking about pictures has been in large measure shaped by Ernst Gombrich, I was fifteen when I read *The Story of Art* and like millions since, I felt I had been given a map of a great country, and with it the confidence to explore further without fear of being overwhelmed.

I hope so personal a beginning may be forgiven in the catalogue of a public exhibition, but it is a striking effect of Gombrich's style that his readers feel they are being personally addressed, engaged, if not quite in a dialogue, then in a kind of individual tutorial. These tutorials have ranged widely in subject, but have repeatedly returned to questions of perception, about how we organise information gained from looking, how we turn sight into insight.

It is a sad truth, repeatedly brought home to us by Gombrich, that most of us can see only what we have already learnt is likely to be there. A botanist will spot distinctions between leaves or petals that escape others, but may in turn miss the details that enthral motor-car enthusiasts. To be observant, we need first to be given something to look for. In this exhibition (generously supported by the Bernard Sunley Foundation), we are looking not for a thing, but its shadow, and a shadow of a particular sort. As soon as the problem is set, we find we can in fact now see and ponder for ourselves what before we had missed: why are shadows only sometimes present, and what is the artist using them to achieve?

It is the mark of the great teachers that they leave us feeling that we have found things out for ourselves. Many of us have, I am sure, put down a Gombrich essay believing that we had been on the verge of that very insight, that we had been standing just behind him, looking over his shoulder on the Darien peak. But we were not. And without him much delight would have remained undiscovered and unconsidered.

This small exhibition is the National Gallery's way of saying thank you to Sir Ernst Gombrich, O M, who has enriched for so many the pleasure to be found in looking at pictures.

Neil MacGregor, Director

Plate 1 Pontormo, *Joseph with Jacob in Egypt*, *c.*1518. Oil on wood, 96.5 x 109.5 cm. London, National Gallery.

ASPECTS OF CAST SHADOWS

THE ART HISTORIAN'S EYE

There is no more dangerous trap set by language than the temptation to take metaphors literally. However gratifying it may be for an art historian to be asked to contribute to a series of exhibitions originally called 'The Artist's Eye', I would still like to remind the reader of the sober fact that neither artists nor art historians have much influence on the quality of their eyes or their eyesight. The eye is an instrument – and what a marvellous instrument – that has evolved over millions of years to enable most organisms endowed with movement to find their way through the world, to recognise their mates, to avoid their enemies or any obstacles in their environment, in short to survive. It is an achievement that depends almost exclusively on the modifications that the surrounding light undergoes when falling on the objects within view. The varieties of light and shade on their surface tell us of their shape, the reflections on that surface indicate its texture, and their reaction to the various wavelengths of the spectrum determine their colour. Clearly, we – no less than the other organisms – are equipped to process and utilise the information we receive without being aware of the underlying mechanism. In that sense we all see the same world and cope with it as best we can.

But so varied and manifold is the information that the eyes are capable of transmitting to our minds that we would be instantly swamped if we had to pay attention to all the messages that reach us from the outside world. Our perception must be, and always is, selective. Thus we can learn, or train ourselves to observe features of our environment which normally bypass our awareness. We are especially likely to do so if such attention serves a particular function, a particular purpose. The earliest hunters probably acquired an 'eye' for the track of bisons in the primeval forest, and the earliest medicine men may have noticed tell-tale symptoms in the behaviour of their patients. That artists, intent on reproducing appearances, also develop a specially sensitive eye for the modifications of light was noted in the ancient world: Cicero remarked that 'painters see more in shadows and protrusions than we ever do'.[1] He was of course living at a time when artists had mastered the surprising skill of simulating appearances by the juxtaposition of pigments on a flat panel or wall. To learn to paint, in such a period, is to learn to pay attention to certain features of our environment that can be used for conjuring up a recognisable image.

What the art historian has trained himself to notice, in his turn, is the selectivity of the painter's 'eye', or rather the range of features artists of different media, schools and periods have chosen to construct their images of the visible world.[2] In seeking to draw attention to this selectivity the exhibition also hopes to clarify the point that we must never assume that artists did not see what they did not paint. The Chinese, for instance, did not normally paint cast shadows, but it would be ludicrous to conclude that they never saw them; at least one instance has come to light where they represented the shadows cast by moonlight, for the simple reason that the poem the painting illustrated mentioned them.[3]

Needless to say, such exceptions are not the concern of this companion volume. It merely wishes to make the reader reflect on the intriguing problem of how and why cast shadows were included and again excluded from the repertory of Western painters. It will have served its purpose all the better if it also helps the reader to acquire an eye for the infinite varieties of light that he can observe both in daytime and in artificial illumination.

Plate 2 Leonie Gombrich, *Shadows cast by a Street Lamp,* 1995.

CAST SHADOWS AND THE LAWS OF OPTICS

I recommend to those who are new to these games the entertainment of watching the gyrations and transformations of their own shadows while walking at night along a lamplit road (Plate 2). As you pass close to the lamp your shadow will appear short and squat by your side, and slowly turn in the direction of your walk while growing longer and narrower, till the bright light of the next lamppost will replace it by the shadow that is now behind you.

We easily understand these transformations as the consequence of two obvious facts – the fact that our bodies are solid and not transparent, and that the rays emanating from what is called a 'point source' are propagated, like all light rays, along straight lines. Draw a line from the lamp to your head and beyond and you can predict the shadow you will cast on the level pavement. If the road goes downhill, of course, the shadow will be correspondingly longer, just as it will be shorter if it goes uphill. If you approach a wall you can watch your shadow creeping up, and should you arrive at a sequence of steps it will be broken up like a concertina.

Not all these observations can be repeated in daylight. Admittedly it may be hard to tell whether I took this photograph of myself (Plate 3)

Plate 3 *Self Portrait of the Author in the Setting Sun.* *c.* 1990. Photograph.

Plate 4 *The Greek Philosopher Anaximander holding a Sundial.* Roman mosaic, 2nd century AD. Trier, Rheinisches Landesmuseum.

under a street lamp or in the setting sun, but if I had used a camcorder the difference would be immediately apparent. I could not have gone nearer or further from the sun since the sun is to all intents and purposes at an infinite distance. Wherever I would have stood on an identical slope in the area, my shadow would have been the same, depending only on the hour of the day and the time of the year, which determine the position of the sun at a given latitude.

The invention of the sundial was based on these invariants and dates back to very ancient times.[4] Various forms of this device were known to classical antiquity (Plate 4), while later centuries introduced further refinements such as the combination of the dial with the marine compass as shown in Holbein's portrait of *'The Ambassadors'* (Plate 5).

Plate 5 Hans Holbein the Younger, *'The Ambassadors'* (detail), 1533. Oil on oak, 207 x 209 cm.
London, National Gallery.

Plate 6 J.M.W. Turner, *Petworth Park; Tillington Church in the Distance, c.*1828. Oil on canvas, 60 x 145.7 cm. London, Tate Gallery.

The calibration of these instruments is complex enough, but the painter who wants to construct the shadows in his field of vision is faced with yet another complication, since he must of course take account of their relevant foreshortening when seen from a given point, as Turner so brilliantly does in his painting of Petworth in evening light (Plate 6). Not that Turner is likely to have measured or constructed these rapidly changing shadows, but the task that he confronted makes us understand why it took such a long time before the theory of shadow construction was fully developed for both artificial light and sunlight.[5]

THE SHADOW IN MYTH AND LEGEND

However much shadows can be shown to obey the simple laws of optics, there is something elusive in their appearance. They are part of our environment but they appear and disappear from sight, they are fugitive and changeable, as any painter will have found who has tried to record their appearance on his canvas. The progression of the sun across the sky, the changes in the cloud cover, must make him envy the photographer who has an instrument which can arrest all such change. We tend to conceive our world as stable, though we are also aware of the varieties of circumstances that may influence the way things look, but even in these circumstances we attribute permanence to the colour or texture of surfaces behind their changing appearance. It is different with shadows because they are not part of the real world. We cannot touch them or grasp them and so ordinary parlance often resorts to the metaphor of shadows to describe anything unreal: shadow boxing is not real boxing and the Shadow Chancellor is not the real chancellor. It was believed by the ancient Greeks that when we take leave of the real world we survive only as shades among shades. And yet there are situations when the appearance of a shadow testifies to the solidity of an object, for what casts a shadow must be real.

There is an enchanting episode in the ancient Indian epic, the *Mahabharata*, telling of the beautiful princess Damayanti and the heroic prince Nala to whom she is to be betrothed. When it comes to the ceremony, however, she finds herself confronted not by one but five Nalas: four gods have been so captivated by her beauty that they have assumed the shape of her chosen beloved. In her distress she utters a prayer and suddenly perceives that of the five identical suitors only one, the real Nala, touches the ground and casts a shadow. The others thus reveal themselves as mere phantoms.

In the West we have the famous story by Adelbert von Chamisso, first published in 1814, of the unhappy Peter Schlemihl who is persuaded by the devil to sell his shadow, with dire consequences. Since he casts no shadow he has lost his place in the real world.

Plate 7 Saenredam after Cornelis Cornelisz., *The Cave of Plato*. Engraving, 1604. London, British Museum.

While in that story the presence of the shadow indicates solid reality, one of the most famous philosophical parables in the Western tradition draws the opposite conclusion. I refer to the passage in Plato's *Republic* where he compares the human condition to that of prisoners so fettered in a cave that they can only see the wall opposite its opening.[6] Consequently they come to regard the shadows cast by the events outside on the wall of the cave as reality till they are enabled to turn round and to recognise their error. The engraving by Saenredam gives an elaborate Christianised interpretation of the passage, singling out some of the features Plato described such as the bearers on the wall carrying 'all sorts of articles... made of stone or wood', which are here turned into images of personifications (Plate 7).

Plato reminded his readers of the tricks of shadow players or puppet shows, for in fact the philosopher looked askance at the illusions created by painters, notably the scene-painters who managed to deceive the senses and to present us with a phantom world. It appears that the Greek term used for illusionistic painting was in fact *skiagraphia*, shadow painting, though it is hard to decide whether the term implied the actual rendering of shadows or merely the use of light and shade for the purpose of modelling (see Plate 4).[7] It was this latter device that revolutionised the art of painting and was destined to become the distinguishing mark of the Western tradition. Neither the art of Egypt nor Greek vase paintings of the early fifth century show signs of modelling or shading, but after the invention of this technique it was never wholly discarded in the West.[8] It was different with cast shadows, which seem to have come and gone, very much like our shadows when walking along a lamplit road.

OBSERVATIONS ON CAST SHADOWS IN THE HISTORY OF PAINTING

The reader must not expect this introduction – designed primarily to illustrate the selectivity of the painter's eye – to offer a coherent history of cast shadows in art. Indeed it will have served its purpose if it stimulates the reader to look for more cast shadows in works of the past and to appreciate their relative rarity. However splendid the modelling in some of the paintings, the represented objects frequently cast no or merely rudimentary shadows on their surroundings.

We soon realise that some of the greatest observers of nature appear to have deliberately avoided the cast shadow. However rich their palette and their mastery of tone and colour, they show us a shadowless world. It looks indeed as if many of these masters had studiously avoided inserting such shadows, as if they regarded them as a disturbing and distracting element in an otherwise coherent and harmonious composition.

That this opinion was widespread among painters of the High Renaissance in Italy is not only evident from the pictures themselves. It can also be proved by an impeccable literary testimony – a passage in Leonardo da Vinci's *Notes*, known as the *Trattato della Pittura*, that could not be more explicit.

Light too conspicuously cut off by shadows is exceedingly disapproved of by painters. Hence, to avoid such awkwardness when you depict bodies in open country, do not make your figures appear illuminated by the sun, but contrive a certain amount of mist or of transparent cloud to be placed between the object and the sun and thus – since the object is not harshly illuminated by the sun – the outlines of the shadows will not clash with the outlines of the lights.[9]

Mark that Leonardo here does not only give his own opinion but tells of a universal prejudice among painters against the rendering of harsh shadows in strong sunlight. He does not appear to disagree with his fellow artists but suggests a simple artifice to avoid this awkwardness – the veiling of the sun and the creation of a slightly misty atmosphere. There is no doubt that Leonardo here followed the tendency of his generation to react strongly against the hard-edged clarity of Quattrocento paintings. Indeed, the section of the *Trattato* devoted to Light and Shade, that occupies no less than 67 pages of the original manuscript (the *Codex Urbinas*), is less concerned with the fall of light from a point source such as a candle or even the sun than it is with the

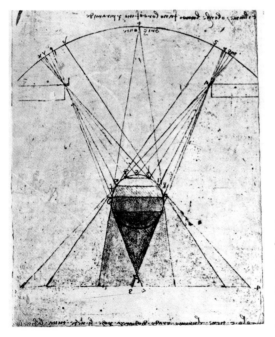

Plate 8 Leonardo, *Codex Urbinas*, c.1490–2. Diagram of light falling on a wall opposite a window, indicating the arc of the horizon and the resulting shadow.
(MS Bibliothèque Nationale 2038 13b)

diffuse light reflected from the sky and the various gradations of tone resulting from indirect light (Plate 8).[10]

What is strange is that Leonardo, the most innovative master of chiaroscuro effects, apparently did not embody in his own paintings the varieties of shadows he had studied so meticulously in his writings. However, some of them had been depicted by the painters of an earlier generation, before, that is, the rendering of shadows appears to have become unfashionable.

Thus it is in the paintings of the first decades of the fifteenth century, both north and south of the Alps, that the effects that interest us can be most frequently observed. Masaccio's fresco representing the episode from the life of Saint Peter when the shadow cast by the saint healed a cripple (Plate 9) stands as a landmark in our story. Such an

Plate 9 Masaccio, *Saint Peter's Shadow Healing,* 1425. Fresco. Florence, Brancacci Chapel.

Plate 10 Workshop of Robert Campin, *The Virgin and Child in an Interior* (detail), *c.*1435. Oil on oak, painted surface 18.7 x 11.6 cm. London, National Gallery.

Plate 11 Attributed to Campin, *The Trinity*, 1427–32. Grisaille. Frankfurt, Städelsches Kunstinstitut.

event could hardly have been rendered in the idiom of Masaccio's predecessors. We can also document the wealth of relevant observations in a painting from the workshop of a northern contemporary, *The Virgin and Child in an Interior* (Plate 10). Even more astounding, however, is the altar wing attributed to the same master representing

Plate 12 Fra Angelico, *The Virgin and Child* (detail), *c*.1450.
Fresco. Florence, San Marco.

a fictitious sculpture of the Trinity standing in a niche and casting two
shadows of different intensities on the wall (Plate 11). Such a refine-
ment would certainly have pleased Leonardo, as he must also have
admired the fresco by Fra Angelico in the cloisters of San Marco in
Florence with the immensely subtle cast shadows of the pilasters' capi-
tals caused by grazing light (Plate 12).

It is not the intention of this rapid survey of the history of our topic
to steal the thunder of the subsequent section that must be devoted to
the choice of examples in the exhibition, but we cannot here bypass

Plate 13 Caravaggio, *The Supper at Emmaus*, 1601. Oil and tempera on canvas, 141 x 196.2 cm. London, National Gallery.

the leading master whose great painting of the *Supper at Emmaus* (Plate 13) is a pivotal work. There is hardly a function of cast shadows that is not illustrated by Caravaggio's dramatic painting, but for that very reason it might also help to explain why so many of the artists of the Cinquecento withheld their attention from cast shadows. Clearly the shadow cast by Christ's blessing hand and arm across his body might have been felt by traditionalists to disrupt the even modelling of the figure, just as the harsh shadows on the tablecloth might have been thought to interfere with the clarity of the composition.[11] Needless to say, many artists of the seventeenth century were rapidly converted to Caravaggio's idiom, and the *tenebroso* (dark) style conquered not only parts of Italy but also whole regions of the north where it culminated in the art of Rembrandt.

The lightening of the palette which we associate with the eighteenth century favoured a return to even illumination, but the *vedutisti* of Venice, such as Guardi (Plate 14), rarely followed Leonardo's advice of hiding the sun behind a veil.

Even before the end of the eighteenth century, observations of the variety of light effects in the open air had led to fresh interest in the colour of shadows[12] which were particularly eagerly studied by the Impressionists. By the end of the ninetenth century, however, the wave

Plate 14 Francesco Guardi, *Venice: The Arsenal* (detail), 1755–60. Oil on canvas, 62.3 x 96.9 cm. London, National Gallery.

Plate 15 Giorgio de Chirico, *The Enigma of a Day*, 1914. Oil on canvas, 83 x 130 cm. Brazil, Museu de Arte Contemporânea da Universidade de Sâo Paulo.

of Japanese influence appears to have demonstrated to the West that shadows could be easily dispensed with in the interest of decorative compositions. Whereas the Fauves reduced tonal modelling to a minimum, Cubism reinstated the role of shadows both to guide and confuse the viewer. Later still the Surrealists exploited the effect of shadows to enhance the mood of mystery they sought, as in De Chirico's dreamlike visions of deserted city squares, where the harsh shadows cast by the statue and solitary figures add to the sense of disquiet (Plate 15).

ARTISTIC FUNCTIONS OF CAST SHADOWS ILLUSTRATED BY PAINTINGS IN THE NATIONAL GALLERY

Plate 16
Giovanni
Battista Moroni,
*Portrait of a
Gentleman*,
*c.*1555–60.
Oil on canvas,
185.4 x 99.7 cm.
London,
National Gallery.

In wishing to draw attention to the variety of artistic functions which cast shadows can serve and have served, we are aware of the pitfalls of any such systematic arrangement, and there are few paintings in any one category of this exhibition that might not have been used in another section.

We have placed at the opening of the series a portrait by Moroni (Plate 16) that beautifully exemplifies both the traditional art of modelling in light and shade, particularly in the rounding of the column, and also the cast shadow of the body on the floor and wall. The example is intended to emphasise again the vital distinction between modelling and cast shadows – the first being universal in Western art (see Plate 4), the second strangely exceptional.

How deeply ingrained in the practice of painting these two resources remain may also be illustrated by an early still life by Picasso (Plate 17) in which the erstwhile student of the academic tradition skilfully observes the rules of modelling and also marks the cast shadows

Plate 17 Pablo Picasso, *Fruit-bowl with Pears and Apples*, 1908. Oil on panel, 27 x 21 cm. On loan from the Berggruen Collection.

thrown by the fruits outside the bowl on the table with a few impatient brushstrokes.

An exhibition devoted to the theme of cast shadows could not well omit the once popular subject of the 'invention of painting', which attributed the origin of the art of portraiture to the observation and tracing of a shadow. Hence the inclusion of the painting by David Allan (Plate 18). The version of this poetic tale told by the Roman encyclopaedist Pliny the Elder takes the form of a love story: Boutades, a potter of Skyon, discovered with the help of his daughter how to model portraits in clay. She was in love with a youth, and when he was leaving the country she traced the outline of the shadow which his face cast on the wall by lamplight. Her father filled in the outline with clay and made a model. The ancient author refers to this legend in his chapter on sculpture rather than painting.[13] It may be that portraits in profile were more familiar on coins and early tomb sculpture than in painting.

Plate 18
David Allan,
*The Origin of Painting
(The Maid of Corinth)*,
1775. Oil on wood,
38.7 x 31 cm. Edinburgh,
National Gallery of
Scotland.

It seems a plausible story, but trying the trick we find that we easily run into difficulty: our own shadow tends to get in the way and obliterates the outlines we wish to draw. Even if we keep our bodies out of the way, the shadow cast by our own drawing hand must inevitably fall precisely on the area we wish to trace.

Of course, human ingenuity can surmount this problem and it did so in the eighteenth century when the cut-out portrait silhouettes became all the rage. The technique was based on the device of letting the shadow fall on a transparent paper and tracing it from the other side (Plate 19). The accuracy secured by this method also gave rise to the vogue of physiognomics, which purported to read the character of a person from the record of a profile.

We must not expect the precision of outline that can be achieved by parallel projection to occur in paintings which serve a very different purpose. Indeed it is only occasionally that artists represented the shadows of objects cast on a vertical wall. We have mentioned that

Plate 19 Drawing of a silhouette, from the English edition of J.C. Lavater's *Physiognomische Fragmente*, London 1797.

marvel of observation, from Campin's workshop, *The Virgin and Child in an Interior* (Plates 20 and 21). Here the artist shows us the fireplace complete with the shadow of the firetongs presumably cast by the light from the flames, and the shutter, cloth and pillow throwing their shadows on the wall in the diffuse light that comes from the window and thus reinforcing the effect of modelling in light and shade in which the master excels.

We may find a similar reinforcement in the art of portraiture as practised north of the Alps. Both the German Master of the Mornauer Portrait (Plate 22) and Hans Holbein (Plate 23) placed the model in full frontal light and allowed their shadows and that of the frame to be visible on the wall behind them. We may not necessarily notice these vague shapes, but they still add to the sense of presence of the sitters.

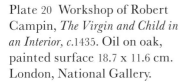

Plate 20 Workshop of Robert Campin, *The Virgin and Child in an Interior, c.*1435. Oil on oak, painted surface 18.7 x 11.6 cm. London, National Gallery.

Plate 21 Detail of Plate 20.

Plate 22 Master of the Mornauer Portrait, *Portrait of Alexander Mornauer*, *c*.1464–88. Oil on wood, original painted surface 45.2 x 38.7 cm. London, National Gallery.

Plate 23 Hans Holbein
the Younger, *Christina of
Denmark, Duchess of Milan*,
probably 1538. Oil on oak,
179.1 x 82.6 cm.
London, National Gallery.

Plate 24 Giovanni Battista Tiepolo,
Saints Augustine, Louis of France, John the Evangelist and a Bishop Saint,
before 1737. Oil on canvas, 58.1 x 33.3 cm.
London, National Gallery.

As a further example of this device we have chosen Tiepolo's sketch for an altar painting (Plate 24) in which the king's hand with the sceptre is beautifully thrown into relief by the clear shadow.

If parallel projection is comparatively rare, the effect of what has been called the 'attached shadow' has always belonged to the resources

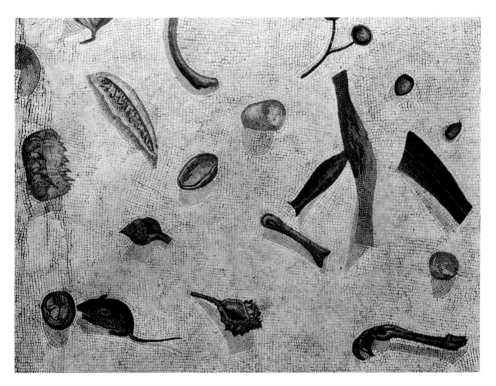

Plate 25 Copy by Heraclitus (2nd century AD) after Sosos of Pergamon, *Scraps of a Meal ('The Unswept Room')*. Detail of mosaic fragment. Rome, Vatican Museums.

of *trompe l'oeil*. The shadow cast by an object on the ground on which it rests immediately enhances the impression of its solidity.

Roman mosaicists sometimes tease the eye by showing an apparently 'unswept floor' (*asaraton*), as it would appear after a banquet, with all the odds and ends scattered about and throwing strong shadows on the pavement (Plate 25).

Plate 26 Antonello da Messina, *Christ Blessing*, c.1465.
Oil on wood, painted surface 38.7 x 29.8 cm.
London, National Gallery.

As soon as shadows re-entered the repertory of painting this unfailing effect of attached shadows was exploited. The *cartellino*, such as the piece of paper with the signature of Antonello da Messina (Plate 26), is a typical instance, and so is the trick of painting a fly on the picture, as in the fifteenth-century portrait of a woman by a Swabian artist (Plate 27), a trick to which André Chastel devoted a special study.[14]

Plate 27 Unknown Swabian Artist, *Portrait of a Woman of the Hofer Family*, *c.*1470. Oil on silver fir, 53.7 x 40.8 cm. London, National Gallery.

Plate 28 Rembrandt,
Portrait of Jan Cornelisz. Sylvius.
Etching, 1646.
London, British Museum.

Plate 29 Caravaggio,
The Supper at Emmaus (detail),
1601. Oil and tempera on
canvas, 141 x 196.2 cm.
London, National Gallery.

Plate 30 Gerrit Berckheyde, *The Marketplace and the Grote Kerk at Haarlem*,
1674. Oil on canvas, 51.8 x 67 cm.
London, National Gallery.

After the taboo on harsh shadows was lifted in the seventeenth
century the device was practised with relish in many contexts. The din-
ing table of Caravaggio's *Supper at Emmaus* (Plate 29) almost rivals the
trick of the ancient mosaic, and Rembrandt's etching of the portrait of
Jan Sylvius (Plate 28) unashamedly uses the device in a medium that
excludes deception.

The strong attached shadows in the paintings by Berckheyde
(Plate 30) and Guardi (Plate 31) surely add to the impression of depth,

Plate 31 Francesco Guardi, *Venice: The Arsenal*, 1755–60.
Oil on canvas, 62.3 x 96.9 cm.
London, National Gallery.

but they also help to enhance the effect of the sunlight flooding the market place and square.

Here is a striking example of the need to look at the paintings illustrated here from various points of view, as few functions of cast shadows are more vital than the possibility of enhancing the impression of light. Since the gamut of tones that is available to the painter encompasses only a fraction of the range of intensities to be observed in nature,[15] he must exploit the effects of tonal contrasts by carefully contrived juxtapositions.

We can see an early and striking example of this possibility in the great painting of the *Virgin and Child* by Masaccio (Plate 32). By representing the shadows falling on the throne Masaccio makes us sense the light that illuminates the whole scene that he has so carefully constructed in perspective. His example is admirable precisely because of the discretion with which he uses this novel resource, which we have also noted in the painting by Robert Campin (see Plate 20).

Plate 32
Masaccio, *The Virgin and Child*, 1426. Tempera on poplar, painted surface 135.5 x 73 cm. London, National Gallery.

Plate 33 Follower of Rembrandt, *A Man seated reading at a Table in a Lofty Room*, *c.*1631–50. Oil on oak, 55.1 x 46.5 cm.London, National Gallery.

What was called the *tenebroso* style of the seventeenth century that we connect with Caravaggio frequently went to extremes to enhance the radiance of light by means of tonal contrast. The painting of a hermit or scholar reading at a table by a follower of Rembrandt or his school (Plate 33) illustrates this effect to perfection. The light streaming through the glass panes and the open window almost dazzles the beholder, making it hard to discover the figure and the objects.

Plate 34 Giovanni
Domenico Tiepolo,
*The Procession of the Trojan
Horse into Troy*, *c*.1760. Oil
on canvas, 38.8 x 66.7 cm.
London, National Gallery.

Plate 35 Jean-Baptiste-Camille Corot, *Peasants under the Trees at Dawn*, *c*.1840–5.
Oil on canvas, 28.2 x 39.7 cm. London, National Gallery.

There is no such 'glaring contrast' in Giovanni Domenico Tiepolo's
vision of the Trojan Horse (Plate 34) but the strong shadows on the
ground also enhance the impression of bright sunlight.

Corot (Plate 35), on the other hand, softens the shadow of the
fallen tree and of the goose and thus convincingly suggests the mellow
light of morning or evening. His painting therefore also illustrates the
creation of a particular mood by means of shadows notably, of course,

(above) Plate 38 Antonello da Messina, *Saint Jerome in his Study* (detail), *c.*1475. Oil on lime, 45.7 x 36.2 cm. London, National Gallery.

(left) Plate 36 Claude, *A Seaport,* 1639. Oil on canvas, 99.1 x 129.5 cm. London, National Gallery.

(below left) Plate 37 Camille Pissarro, *Fox Hill, Upper Norwood,* 1870. Oil on canvas, 35.5 x 45.7 cm. London, National Gallery.

the lengthening of shadows caused by the rising or setting sun which is so memorably depicted by Claude in his harbour scene (Plate 36).

The Impressionists laid increasing stress on the observation that shadows are rarely grey but exhibit varying hues due to their contrast with the colours of their environment. The winter landscape by Pissarro (Plate 37) illustrates this point.

Not only the shape but also the outer limits of the shadows and their colour can convey to us the character of the illuminating light, and again we find astoundingly early examples of such observations in the art of the early fifteenth century. Fra Angelico's feat of rendering the *sfumato* of grazing light (see Plate 12) was mentioned earlier. The National Gallery possesses another no less striking example, Antonello da Messina's *Saint Jerome in his Study* (Plate 38), notably the shadow of the peacock falling on the steps with its *sfumato* outline.

Antonello's painting also reminds us of the skill needed to depict shadows falling on an irregular background. We find another early

Plate 39 Sassetta, *The Stigmatisation of Saint Francis*, 1437–44. Tempera on poplar, 87.5 x 52.5 cm. London, National Gallery.

Plate 40 Carlo Crivelli, *The Annunciation*
(detail), 1486. Egg and oil on canvas
transferred from wood, 207 x 146.7 cm.
London, National Gallery.

Plate 41 Pontormo, *Joseph with Jacob in
Egypt* (detail), *c.*1518. Oil on wood,
painted surface 96.5 x 109.5 cm.
London, National Gallery.

example in Sassetta's *Stigmatisation of Saint Francis* (Plate 39) where the
complex shadow behind the kneeling saint is caused by the radiance
emanating from the apparition in the sky.

Crivelli achieves a similar effect in his painting of *The Annunciation*
(Plate 40) where the angel and the bishop cast a shadow on the floor
and wall.

A virtuoso piece in this mode is surely the group of shadows in
Pontormo's multiple composition of the story of Joseph (Plate 41)

where the figures mounting the curving stairs cast carefully calculated shadows on the round wall behind them.

Effects of this kind are most often observed in the strong shadows cast by artificial light, and indeed in *The Concert* (Plate 42) ter Brugghen shows us a conspicuous shadow thrown by the flute on the cheek of the player illuminated by the candle in the centre. In Rembrandt's *Adoration of the Shepherds* (Plate 43) such virtuosity serves the mood of the holy story: the light radiating from the Child does not quite eclipse the light of the lantern falling on the floor of the stable.

Plate 42 Hendrick ter Brugghen, *The Concert*, c.1626.
Oil on canvas, 99.1 x 116.8 cm.
London, National Gallery.

Plate 43 Rembrandt, *The Adoration of the Shepherds*, 1646.
Oil on canvas, 65.5 x 55 cm.
London, National Gallery.

Plate 44 Jacob van Ruisdael, *An Extensive Landscape with a Ruined Castle and a Village Church*, *c*.1665–70. Oil on canvas, 109 x 146 cm. London, National Gallery.

The Dutch landscape painters of the seventeenth century also knew how to enhance the feeling of wide vistas by showing shadows cast by heavy clouds on irregular terrain (Plate 44).

The interior of a church by Emanuel de Witte (Plate 45) finally reminds us of the capacity of shadows to reveal part of a scene that lies hidden from the viewer. We observe on the wall in front of us patterns of sunlight projected through the unseen windows on the opposite side of the nave.

William Collins, an anecdotal painter of the nineteenth century, cunningly appealed to the imagination of the beholder in his painting *Coming Events* (Plate 46),[16] by the device of the shadow of the unseen object. The painting shows a country lad who has just opened the gate and touches his cap – to whom? To the horseman whose shadow we see in the foreground.

Plate 45 Emanuel de Witte, *The Interior of the Oude Kerk, Amsterdam, during a Sermon*, c.1660. Oil on canvas, 51.1 x 56.2 cm. London, National Gallery.

Plate 46 William Collins, *Coming Events*, 1833. Oil on canvas, 71 x 91.5 cm. Chatsworth, Devonshire collection.

Plate 47 Henri Cartier-Bresson, *India, Ahmedabad*, 1967.

To us these paintings may look somewhat contrived, but the photographer, who likes to take pictures with the sun behind him, will often detect in his rangefinder tell-tale shadows of objects outside his field of vision.[17] It is hard to imagine a more poignant use of this device than Cartier-Bresson's photograph from India (Plate 47) showing the exhausted sleeper sheltering from the sun in the shadow of an elaborate shrine.

Whether or not Gauguin was influenced by photography in this respect, it is interesting to note that he considered this use the only legitimate one. Citing the Japanese, who could do so well without light and shade, he was inclined to 'do away' with shadows which serve illusionism. 'If, instead of a figure, you put the shadow only of a person', he wrote to Emile Bernard in 1888, 'you have found an original starting point, the strangeness of which you have calculated.'[18]

More than twenty years earlier, the French salon painter Gérôme had achieved considerable notoriety with his vision of Golgotha (Plate 48), showing just the shadows of the three crosses against a dramatically lit landscape. As a Symbolist, Gauguin would probably also have

Plate 48 Jean-Leon Gérôme, *Golgotha: Consummatum est*, 1867.
Oil on canvas, 63.5 x 98 cm. Paris, Musée d'Orsay.

Plate 49 William Holman Hunt, *The Shadow of Death*, 1870–3.
Oil on canvas, 214.2 x 168.2 cm.
Manchester City Art Galleries.

accepted the use of shadows to reveal a prophecy of things to come. In this vein Holman Hunt had turned the shadow of the youthful Christ into a portent of His ultimate death on the cross (Plate 49).

These examples still retain the required resemblance between the object and its shadow, but we also know that shadows can be manipulated to suggest what is not there. Anybody who has ever amused a child with the trick of conjuring up with his hands the shadow of a rabbit wriggling its ears need not be told of this possibility, but these tricks would find a more natural place in the Museum of the Moving Image. What creates the striking effect in the manipulated shadow is the possibility of animating the shape and of distorting it in the most unexpected ways. We have seen that shadow performances are men-

Plate 50 Samuel van Hoogstraten, *Shadow Theatre*. From *Inleyding tot de hooghe schoole der schilderkonst* 1678.

tioned as early as the fourth century BC by Plato (see page 18), and this art was never forgotten since it proved particularly suitable for the evocation of ghost stories, demons and hobgoblins. The illustration by Hoogstraten (Plate 50) of such a fantastic show on mythological themes making use of the effect of footlights may, but need not be, wholly fictitious. Indeed, shortly before the arrival of photography and the movies such displays were very much in vogue in France, where one even spoke of *ombremanie*.[19]

These developments surely fall outside the purview of this book, but it may well conclude by reminding the reader of images that may have drawn their original inspiration from such entertainments and harnessed the real or manipulated shadow to the service of moral instruction or satire.

Thus Otto van Veen in a seventeenth-century emblem book transforms the shadow of Cupid into a sinister apparition to point the moral that love engenders envy (Plate 51). While the nineteenth-century caricaturist Grandville harks back to the fashion of the silhouette portrait

Plate 51 Otto van Veen, *The Shadow of Cupid.*
Engraving from *Amorum Emblemata*, Antwerp 1608, p. 51.

Plate 52 Grandville, *The Shadows (The French Cabinet)* from *La Caricature*, 1830.

that was our starting point in order to make the shadows thrown on a wall by members of the French Cabinet (Plate 52) reveal their true natures – a drunkard, a devil, a swine and a dupe (turkey).

No one will be surprised that examples from this category could not be found among the paintings of the National Gallery, but that cast shadows as such are so comparatively rare among its treasured masterpieces was perhaps worth pointing out. I hope this companion volume will encourage the visitor to make his own tour of the Gallery and seek out his own examples.

NOTES

1. 'Quam multa vident pictores in umbris et eminentia quae nos non videmus' (Cicero, *Accademica* II. 20, 86).
2. I have dealt with another aspect of this selectivity in my chapter 'Light, Form and Texture in 15th Century Painting North and South of the Alps', *The Heritage of Apelles*, Oxford 1976, pp. 19–38.
3. This painting is reproduced in the catalogue of *Chinese Calligraphy and Painting in the Collection of John M. Crawford, JR.* (New York 1962): it is by Ch'iao Chung-ch'ang (active in the first half of the twelfth century) and illustrates the passage of a prose poem which reads: 'When we passed the slope of Huang-ni the frost and dew had fallen already. The trees were stripped of leaves, our shadows were on the ground; we looked up at the full moon, enjoyed its radiance around us...' James Cahill, who wrote the catalogue entry, very kindly drew my attention to this exceptional case.
4. See the entry under Dial in the *Encyclopaedia Britannica*; see also René R.J. Rohr, *Die Sonnenuhr*, Munich 1984.
5. Thomas Da Costa Kaufmann, 'The Perspective of Shadows: The History of the Theory of Shadow Projection', *Journal of the Warburg and Courtauld Institutes*, Vol. 38, 1975, pp. 258–87.
6. Plato, *The Republic*, VII, 514–15.
7. Ernst Pfuhl, *Die Malerei und Zeichnung der Griechen*, Munich 1923, and M.H. Swindler, *Ancient Painting*, New Haven 1929.
8. See the title essay of *The Heritage of Apelles*, cited in note 2.
9. Leonardo da Vinci, *Treatise on Painting*, ed. A. Philip McMahon, Princeton 1956, p. 70 (Codex Urbinas 40 v.).
10. Copies or variants of other shadow studies by Leonardo appear to be preserved in the Codex Huygens. See Erwin Panofsky, ed., *The Codex Huygens*, London 1940.
11. There are many passages in early painting manuals warning against the disruptive effect of shadows, particularly the cast shadows thrown by one figure onto another, and emphasising the importance of harmony and unity. See Vasari, *Le Vite*, ed. G. Milanesi, Milan 1878–85, Vol.I, p.180.
12. For coloured shadows see the letter from the physicist Lichtenberg to Goethe of 1793 that I cited in *The Image and the Eye*, Oxford 1982, p. 30.
13. Pliny, *Historia Naturalis*, XXXV, 151.
14. André Chastel, 'Musca depicta', FMR 1984.
15. See Chapter 1 of my *Art and Illusion*, Oxford 1960.
16. See the entry for 'Rustic Civility', a smaller replica of the painting, in the V&A Museum *Catalogue of British Oil Paintings 1820–1860* by Ronald Parkinson, London 1990, p. 36.
17. For shadows in photography see M. Luckiesh, 'The Cast Shadow' in *Light and Shadow and their Applications*, New York 1916. For the simulated shadows of computer graphics see William J. Mitchell, *The Reconfigured Eye*, Cambridge, Mass. 1992. See also *L'Ombra*, ed. Silvana Sinisi, exh. cat., Casa del Mantegna, Mantua 1979.
18. H.B. Chipp, *Theories of Modern Art*, Berkeley 1968.
19. For the nineteenth-century vogue of shadow displays in France see Michel Melot, *L'Oeuil qui rit*, Fribourg 1975, pp. 102–4.

LIST OF WORKS IN THE EXHIBITION

David Allan
The Origin of Painting
(The Maid of Corinth), 1775
Edinburgh, National Gallery of Scotland
Plate 18

Antonello da Messina
*Christ Blessing, c.*1465
London, National Gallery (NG 673)
Plate 26

Antonello da Messina
*Saint Jerome in his Study, c.*1475
London, National Gallery (NG 1418)
Plate 38

Gerrit Berckheyde
The Marketplace and the Grote Kerk at Haarlem,
1674
London, National Gallery (NG 1420)
Plate 30

Hendrick ter Brugghen
The Concert, 1626
London, National Gallery (NG 6483)
Plate 42

Workshop of Robert Campin
*The Virgin and Child in an Interior, c.*1435
London, National Gallery (NG 6514)
Plates 10, 20 and 21

Claude
A Seaport, 1639
London, National Gallery (NG 5)
Plate 36

William Collins
Coming Events, 1833
Chatsworth, Devonshire Collection
Lent by the Duke of Devonshire and the
Chatsworth Settlement Trustees
Plate 46

Jean-Baptiste-Camille Corot
*Peasants under the Trees at Dawn, c.*1840–5
London, National Gallery (NG 6439)
Plate 35

Carlo Crivelli
The Annunciation, 1486
London, National Gallery (NG 739)
Plate 40

Francesco Guardi
Venice: The Arsenal, 1755–60
London, National Gallery (NG 3538)
Plates 14 and 31

Hans Holbein the Younger
Christina of Denmark, Duchess of Milan,
probably 1538
London, National Gallery (NG 2475)
Plate 23

Masaccio
The Virgin and Child, 1426
National Gallery (NG 3046)
Plate 32

Master of the Mornauer Portrait
*Portrait of Alexander Mornauer, c.*1464–88
London, National Gallery (NG 6532)
Plate 22

Giovanni Battista Moroni
*Portrait of a Gentleman, c.*1555–60
London, National Gallery (NG 1316)
Plate 16

Pablo Picasso
Fruit-bowl with Pears and Apples, 1908
On loan to the National Gallery from the
Berggruen Collection (L 515)
Plate 17

Pontormo
Joseph with Jacob in Egypt, c.1518
London, National Gallery (NG 1131)
Plates 1 and 41

Rembrandt
The Adoration of the Shepherds, 1646
London, National Gallery (NG 47)
Plate 43

Rembrandt
Portrait of Jan Cornelisz. Sylvius, 1646
Etching.
London, The Trustees of the British Museum
Plate 28

Follower of Rembrandt
A Man seated reading at a Table in a Lofty Room,
*c.*1631–50
London, National Gallery (NG 3214)
Plate 33

Jacob van Ruisdael
An Extensive Landscape with a Ruined Castle and
a Village Church, c.1665–70
London, National Gallery (NG 990)
Plate 44

Saenredam after Cornelis Cornelisz.
The Cave of Plato, 1604
Engraving.
London, The Trustees of the British Museum
Plate 7

Sassetta
The Stigmatisation of Saint Francis, 1437–44
London, National Gallery (NG 4760)
Plate 39

Unknown Swabian Artist
Portrait of a Woman of the Hofer Family, c.1470
London, National Gallery (NG 722)
Plate 27

Giovanni Battista Tiepolo
Saints Augustine, Louis of France, John the
Evangelist and a Bishop Saint, before 1737
London, National Gallery (NG 1193)
Plate 24

Giovanni Domenico Tiepolo
The Procession of the Trojan Horse into Troy,
*c.*1760
London, National Gallery (NG 3319)
Plate 34

Emanuel de Witte
The Interior of the Oude Kerk, Amsterdam,
during a Sermon, c.1660
London, National Gallery (NG 1053)
Plate 45

INDEX OF NAMES

PICTURE CREDITS